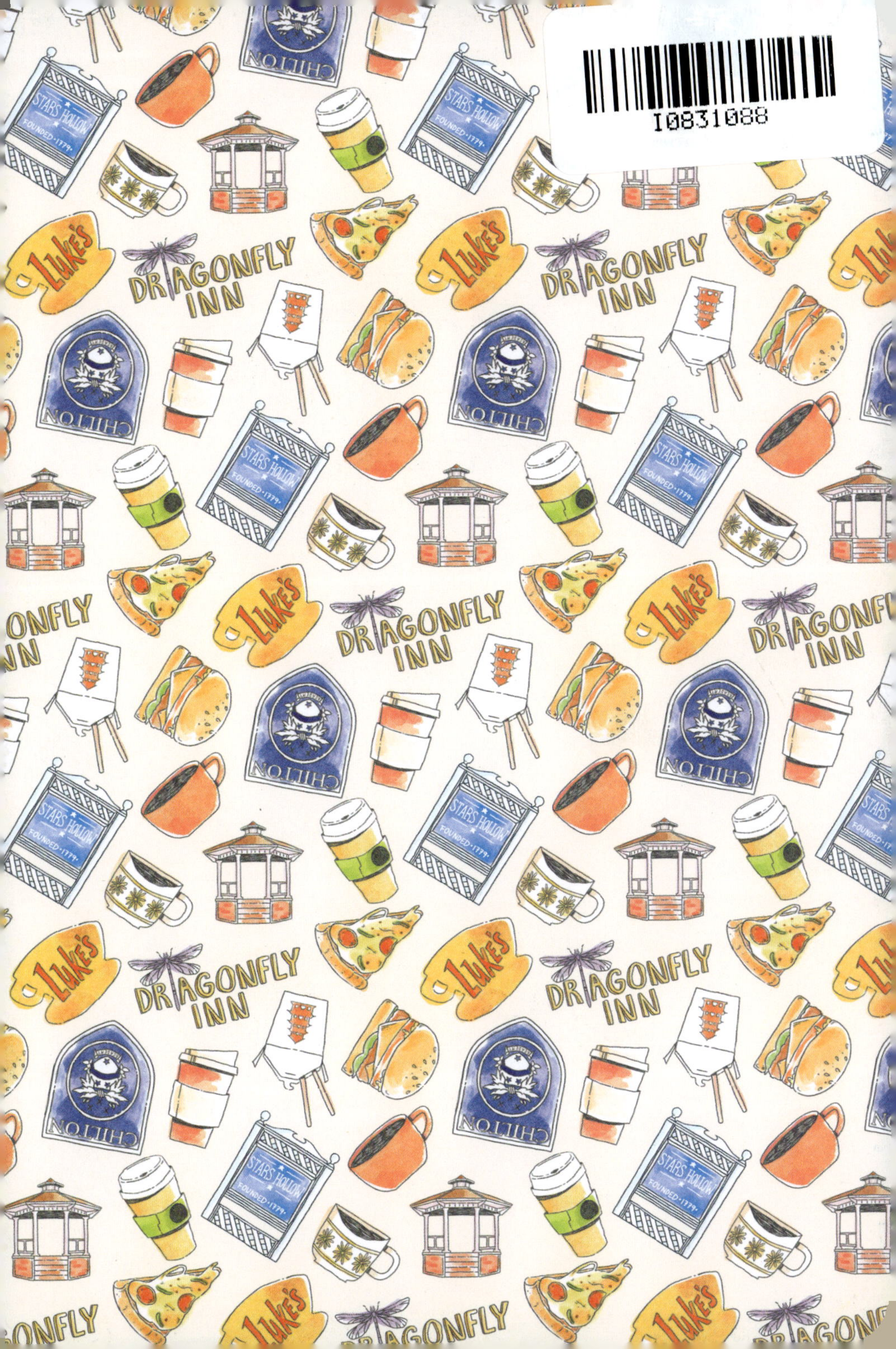
STARS HOLLOW
FOUNDED · 1779 ·
CHILTON
Luke's
DRAGONFLY
INN

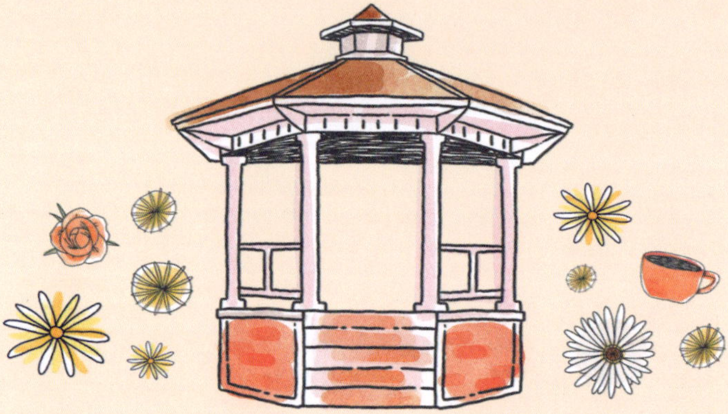

This Journal Belongs To:

Everything in my life has something to do with coffee.
I believe in a former life I was coffee.

—Lorelai Gilmore

Luke's

Luke's

Luke's

I don't like Mondays, but unfortunately,
they come around eventually.

—Lorelai Gilmore

Luke's

Luke's

Luke's

If eating cake is wrong, I don't want to be right.

—Lorelai Gilmore

Luke's

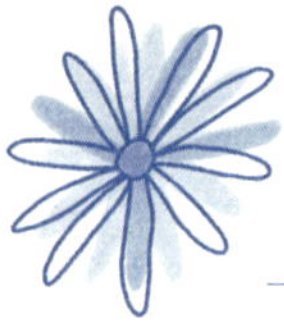

Luke's

Luke's

A little nervous breakdown
can really work wonders for a girl.

—Rory Gilmore

Luke's

Luke's

Luke's

I'm attracted to pie.
It doesn't mean I feel the need to date pie.

—Lorelai Gilmore

Luke's

Luke's

Luke's

I can be flexible, as long as everything is exactly the way I want.

—Lorelai Gilmore

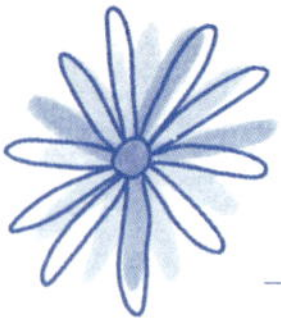

Luke's

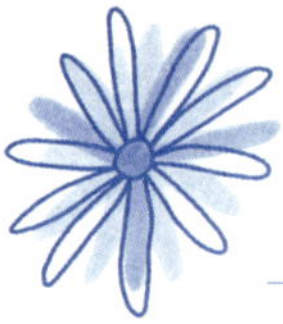

Luke's

Luke's

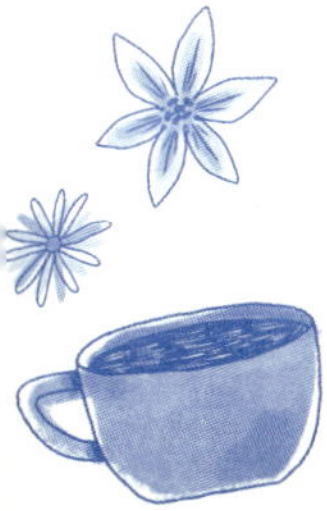

You're full of hate and loathing and I love it.

—Lorelai Gilmore

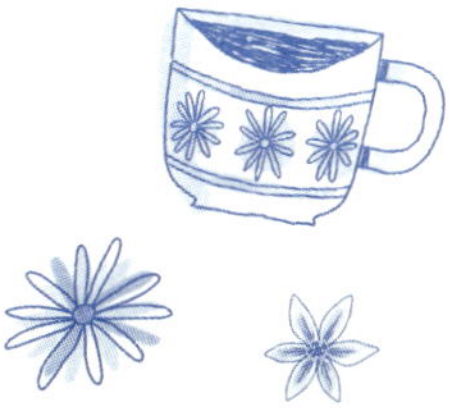

Luke's

Luke's

Luke's

I live in two worlds, one is a world of books.

—Rory Gilmore

Luke's

Luke's

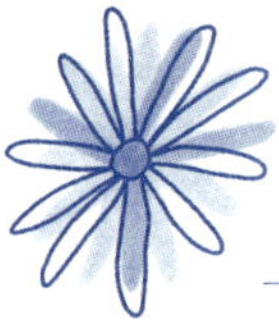

Luke's

We're almost there and nowhere near it.
All that matters is that we're going!

—Lorelai Gilmore

Luke's

Luke's

Luke's

There's plenty to do tonight that
we can be mortified about tomorrow.

—Lorelai Gilmore

Luke's

Luke's

Luke's

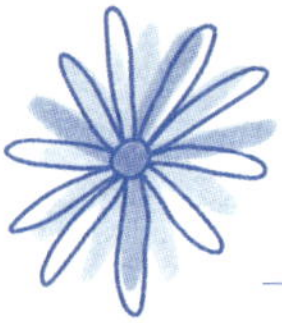

I'm going to have to quit drinking coffee!
And I love coffee—I really love coffee!

—Rory Gilmore

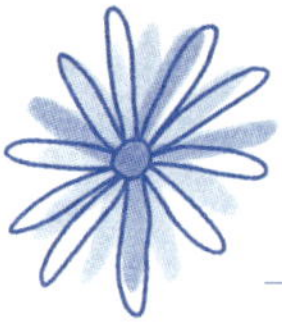

Luke's

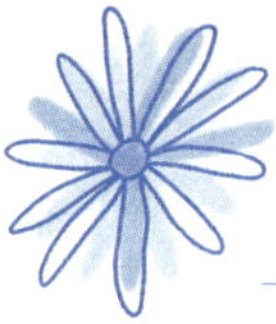

Luke's

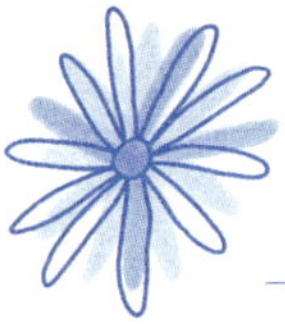

Luke's

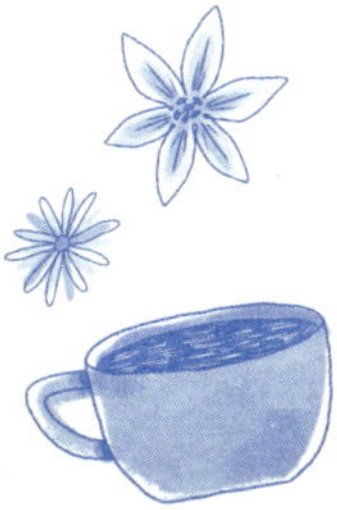

I smell snow!

–Lorelai Gilmore

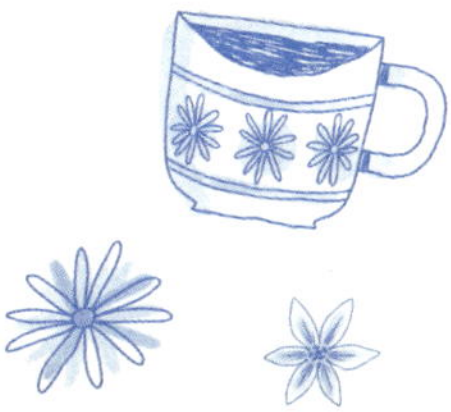

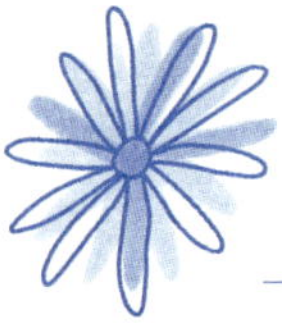

Luke's

Luke's

Luke's

You have so many years of screw-ups ahead of you.

—Lorelai Gilmore

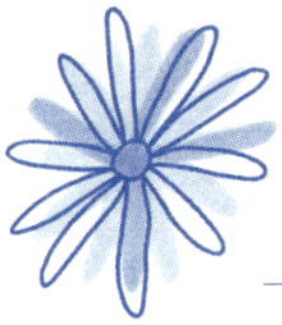

Luke's

Luke's

Luke's

I'm fine. I'm just being dramatic. It's what I do.

—Lorelai Gilmore

Luke's

Luke's

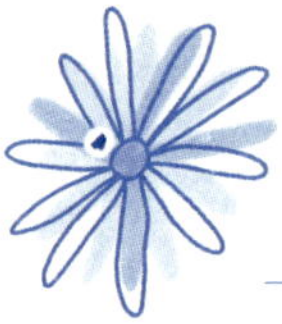

Luke's

This is a jumbo coffee morning. I need coffee in an I.V.

—Lorelai Gilmore

Luke's

Luke's

Luke's

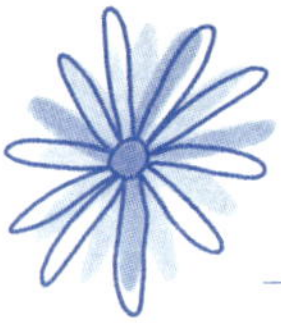

I'm gonna have pancakes with a side of pancakes.

—Lorelai Gilmore

Luke's

Luke's

Luke's

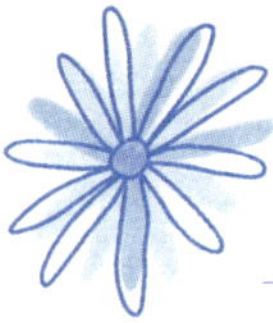

People don't realize it, but it takes years of training to eat the way we do.

—Lorelai Gilmore

Luke's

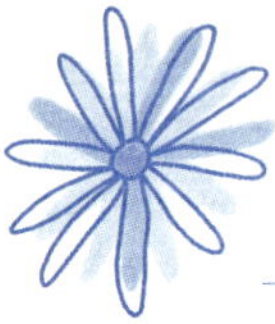

Luke's

Luke's

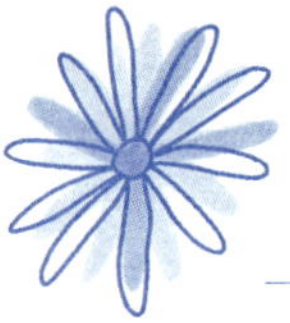

I can't stop drinking the coffee. I stop drinking the coffee,
I stop doing the standing and the walking and
the words putting into sentence doing.

—Lorelai Gilmore

Luke's

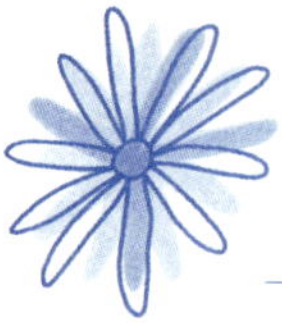

Luke's

Luke's

Who cares if I'm pretty if I fail my finals?!

—Rory Gilmore

Luke's

Luke's

Luke's

Hey, call me crazy, but I just don't think that Butterfingers go with jujubes.

—Rory Gilmore

Luke's

Luke's

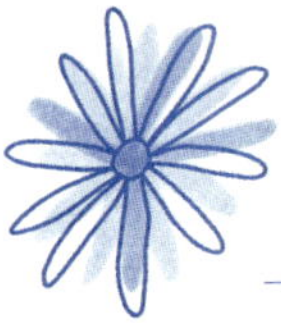

Luke's

Nothing excites me before 11.

—Rory Gilmore

Luke's

Luke's

Luke's

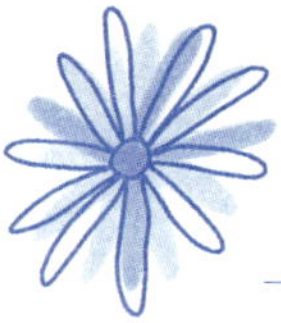

You know my babbling capabilities are infinite.

—Lorelai Gilmore

Luke's

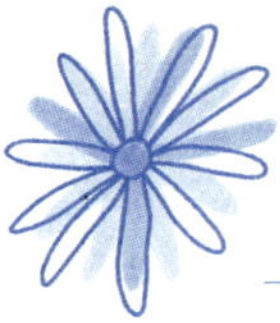

Luke's

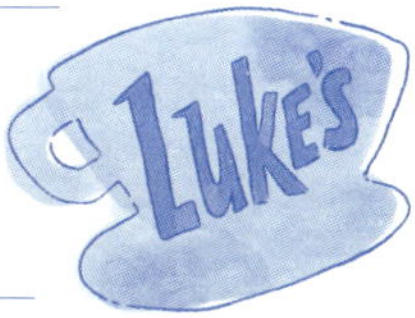
Luke's

I will say anything for a cup of coffee.

—Lorelai Gilmore

Luke's

Luke's

Luke's

You know what I just realized?
Oy is the funniest word in the entire world.

—Lorelai Gilmore

Luke's

Luke's

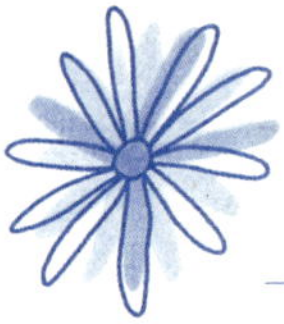

Luke's

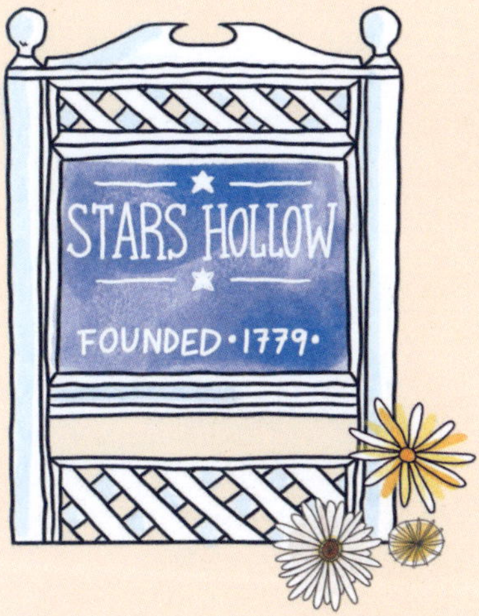

Gilmore girls

INSIGHTS
insighteditions.com

MANUFACTURED IN CHINA
10 9 8 7 6 5 4 3 2

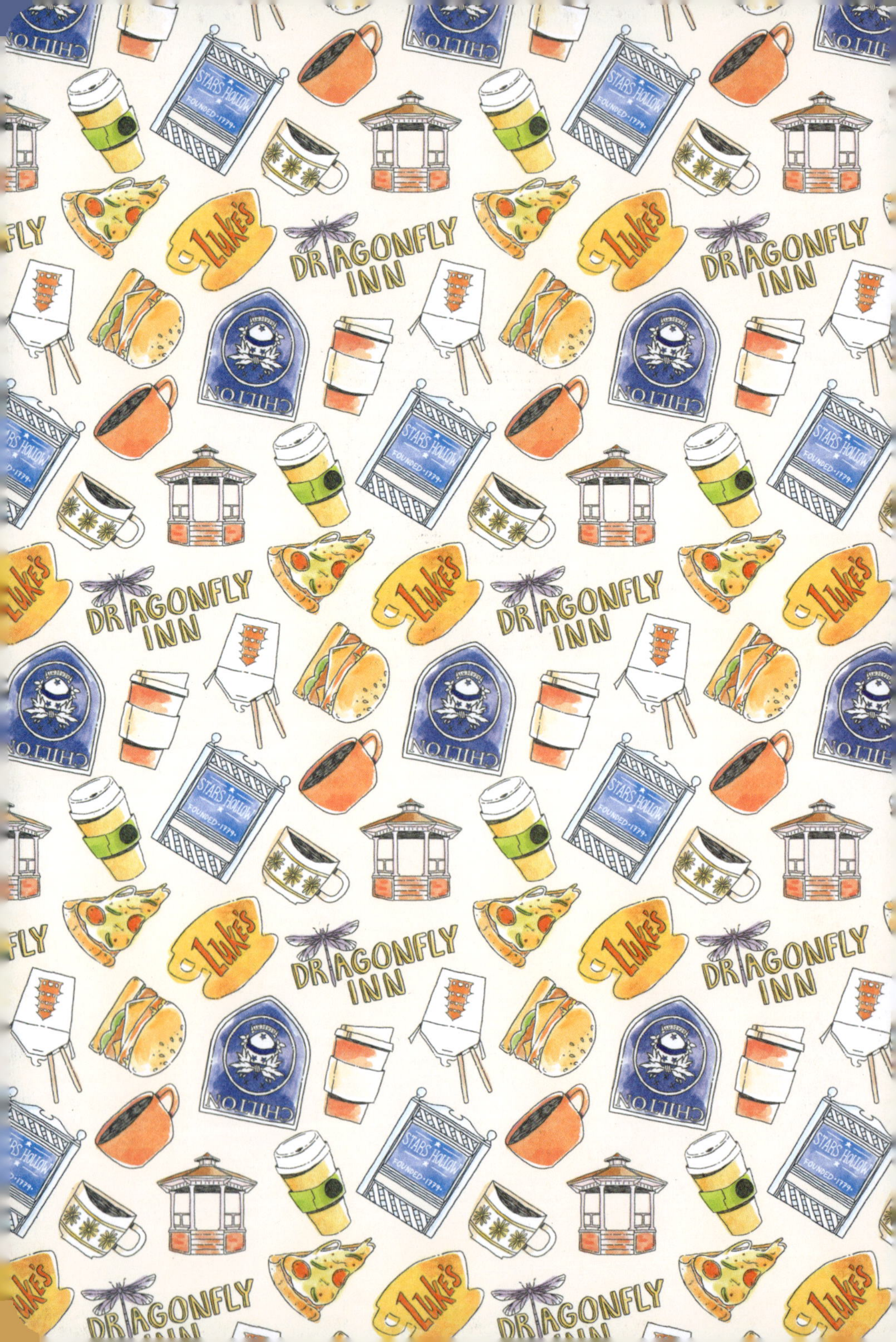
DRAGONFLY INN
Luke's
STARS HOLLOW
FOUNDED 1779
CHILTON